WITLEY AND MILFORD IN LIVING MEMORY:

A COMPILATION OF ORAL AND ARCHIVE MATERIAL ON THE 20th CENTURY FOR THE VILLAGES AND SURROUNDING HAMLETS

BY
VALERIE BOX, BA(Hons)

On behalf of Witley Parish Council,
as part of the celebration of the new millennium

October, 1999

Sherbourne, Petworth Road, Witley, Godalming,
Surrey GU8 5LP.

Published by Witley Parish Council.
November 1999.

ISBN © 095376191-6

Printed by Blackdown Press Limited,
Fernhurst, Haslemere, Surrey GU27 3EE.

Front cover illustration: Painting of the old Post Office, Brook by Helen Allingham.
Reproduced courtesy of Annabel Watts.

Back cover illustration: 'Sister Cottage', Brook.
Reproduced courtesy of Annabel Watts.

Fronticepiece: View of All Saints Church, Witley.
Reproduced courtesy of Roger Egerton.

ACKNOWLEDGEMENTS

Witley Parish Council gratefully acknowledges the assistance of Annabel Watts who generously allowed us to choose from her extensive collection of photographs of Allingham paintings and of the cottages as they are now for the cover illustrations.

This book would not have been possible without the willing co-operation of many present and former residents. Particular thanks go to the local author, Brian Martin, who collated the memories of many of the older residents of Brook and Sandhills, and who largely wrote chapter 3. Angela and Tim Reynolds were instrumental in the collection of material for this section. I am also greatly indebted to Mrs Olwen Heyes of Milford who for over 40 years has been writing down snippets about the village told her by local families. She generously gave me access to her collection, much of which has been used.

Some residents have been interviewed whilst others wrote their recollections: many are mentioned by name in the text. Others include Mrs Coupland, Miss Sylvia Harvey, Miss Evelyn Holmes and Mr Ron Mott. Many others have unwittingly contributed as past conversations have been recalled by the author and past contributions to village magazines have been utilised. I thank them all, and apologize to any who have not been properly acknowledged. In any book like this where oral histories are a significant item, there are bound to be differing versions of events. I have tried to ensure the accuracy of this text wherever possible but apologize for any errors and omissions which can be corrected in any future edition.

I gratefully acknowledge the help of those involved with the exhibitions in All Saints Church in 1995 for access to their records for the contributions attributed to Frank Ashdown and Violet Ford.

Mr Richard Broad, formerly of King Edward's School, allowed me to use his compilations of local history to which the school kindly gave me access. Amongst them was the history of the Canadian Camp during World War I that he compiled from letters and documents lent him by Sergeant White formerly of Milford.

St Thomas' Hospital provided the history of its evacuation to Milford from its book on the history of St Thomas' Hospital. Mrs Noreen Steere and Mrs Pamela Fisher gave us the history of the Chichester Hall. Mrs Phil Murfitt supplied the history of non conformist worship in Milford. The history of Milford Village Hall was supplied by various local residents and also taken from Mr Trevor Clarke's article in the Parish Newsletter in 1995.

Information on Wilfred Owen was taken from his biography, 'Wilfred Owen' by Jon Stallworthy (Oxford University Press, 1974) and from 'The Poems of Wilfred Owen' edited by the same author (Chatto and Windus, 1990).

Mr Percy Childs of Milford generously lent me a private publication, 'What the Butler Heard', written by his relative, Leslie Arthur Bonner (1906-1989) whose father was head gardener on the Enton Estate. Details of life at Enton and Lea Park were taken from this book. Further information on Witley Park was provided by Witley Park Conference Centre. Mr Childs also lent several photos of the area, some of which are reproduced in the text. Other illustrations have been provided by Mr John Young of the Godalming Museum from his extensive private collection and from the Museum's collection on Lea Park. Mr J H Devine of 'Stonehaven' provided information on his house and provided the photograph of 'The Hill'.

Mr W Charles Palmer's 1971 and 1972 private publications, 'Witley Lives', were a valuable source of reference, as were old Parish newsletters and official guides. Information on Rake Manor came from Alan Bott's paper 'Rake Manor, Godalming, Surrey', 1990: Surrey Archaeological Collection, vol 80. Information on Graham Robertson was taken from Annabel Watt's book 'Helen Allingham's Cottage Homes Revisited' published by the author in 1994.

Finally the author wishes to thank Miss Ruth Mullard for correcting some of the text, Mr Hugh Turrall Clarke for his independent review of the complete work and the various members of Witley Parish Council who helped in the production and distribution of this book.

Valerie Box

Contents

All Saints Church, Witley by Mr. R.Q. Egerton. Photographed 1999.

Chapter 1

1900-1914 and The Great War

Witley before the first World War was a close community, with many well established families. The population of the civil parish in 1901 was 2,827. By 1911, boundary changes had made Witley the largest rural parish in the area, with a population of 4,003 inhabitants, whereas Cranleigh's was 3,211.

Miss Cicely Puttick of Milford recalled Queen Victoria's Diamond Jubilee Celebrations in 1897 when villagers gathered in Webb Park behind Milford House for a celebratory tea, at the invitation of Mr R.W. Webb, the village squire. During the celebrations, a lady known as 'Granny Cole' promised to dance with the vicar. It was her 100th birthday that year. Mr Webb also allowed the grounds of Milford House to be used for the annual summer treat for local schoolchildren and for the local flower show, which for many years combined Milford with Witley and Hambledon.

There was plenty to do, partly since everyone walked to wherever they were going and everyday tasks took so long to accomplish without the appliances now taken for granted. Mrs Annie Talman moved into the village in 1913 at the age of 9, and lived in Step Cottage by Witley Church. Her father was church verger and sexton. She remembers going to school across the road until she was 14, when pupils had the option of taking a labour exam before leaving. There were about 70 or 80 children in the school, with the infants in the largest room and four other classes. Drill was performed regularly on the square ground above the school. The head teacher was Mr Wigan who had a love of general knowledge that he endeavoured to impart to his pupils. On Ascension Day, the schoolboys played the choirboys at cricket with Mr Wigan as umpire. On All Saints Day the teams competed at football. Being a Church School, the pupils went to church on these days from nine to ten, but the rest of the day was a holiday. Special dates in the calendar like St George's Day and Empire Day were always celebrated, and on May Day the children danced round the Maypole at Sandhills.

One of the pupils from Witley School became the curator to the largest moth and butterfly collection in the United Kingdom, at the time a private collection at 'Stonehaven' on Wormley Hill. 'Stonehaven' had originally been the artist Birket Foster's ballroom and studio. The collection comprised examples from all over the world, and upon the death of its owner, Mr Joicey, was given to the Natural History Museum.

After school, Witley children would race down the hill to the sweetshop behind the Sun Inn: the first one to arrive always seemed to get the best sweets. There was never more than ½d to spend on aniseed balls or liquorice sticks. If you didn't have any money to spend at Emmie's, then the alternative attraction was watching the horses being shod by the blacksmith at the end of Northfields, on the land that is now George Eliot Close. Horse transport was the only option with the horse taxis or the carrier service the only alternatives to walking. The carrier service operated from Chiddingfold and Hambledon, taking orders to stores like Lipton and Home and Colonial in Godalming for return delivery the same day. Occasionally a travelling hurdy gurdy would stop in the village: definitely one of the highlights.

According to Miss Puttick, the shops in Milford at the turn of the century were few in number. She remembered Burdocks, who were grocers and bakers, and the post office by the Red Lion, where the video shop is now. The village butcher was Rothwell's, occupying the premises on the corner of the crossroads that is now Alldays.

New Road, or Ladycross as it was then known, has always had its own collection of shops. The name 'Ladycross' derives from the small shrines put at crossroads, and in Milford early maps show the original Ladycross was nearer Moushill Lane at the Green Lane crossroads, but by the early 20th century, the name relates to what is now known as New Road.

A small grocer's shop was kept by Mrs Elsley and later by Mr Booker and his daughter Hilda with her husband Henry Leichnitz. Henry and Hilda had a new shop built that is now the dentist and veterinary surgery. The shop now well known as the Surrey Guild of Craftsmen was remembered by Miss Puttick originally as a grocer's, George and William White, later to become Burgess' Stores.

When Mrs Talman was a pupil there, a river ran down the road outside Witley school, known as the River Wit, but it was led underground either

Moushill at the turn of the century

Ladycross, ca 1906

before or during the first war. Another branch of the river ran down the hill parallel to the road, through farmland and down to Roke Lane across where the retirement block, Dorlcote, is situated. This part of the river was a great meeting place in the summer for village children who paddled where it flowed through flatter land before making its way to LeLords pond, opposite the Star at Ditton's Corner. When Dorlcote and the houses in Willowmead were built by the local council in the late 1960s, the river was diverted. By then the pond had already been drained for road safety reasons - too many people had fallen in on the unlit road - and the stream led under the road to ditches the other side. It flows approximately north east, crossing Rake Lane before finally entering into the Ock at Milford.

Another popular bathing place for the children was in the stream from Sweetwater Lake that ran in a tunnel under the railway into a pool called 'The Lagg' in the birch wood. The children bathed without clothes, and delighted in emerging from the tunnel each time a train went by so they could wave to the passengers.

Amongst the colourful characters in the village was the playwright Graham Robertson who lived in 'Sandhills' in Brook Road and who features again in Chapter 3. He was noted for his flamboyant appearance, sporting large Stetson hats, floppy bows and tweedy capes and surrounded by his four large Old English Sheepdogs. During his time in Sandhills he bought Sandhills Common, neighbouring fields and 16 cottages. Many adders were found on the heath, and if any boy brought him a dead adder, he rewarded them with five shillings. He never took the adder, so one snake went through several hands. He later gave the common to the National Trust. The field next to his house was given to the Parish Council and was used for many years as allotments before being turned back to an open green in 1996. Upon his death in 1948, all his cottages were left to their tenants.

The workhouse for the area was in Hambledon and it was a regular occurrence night and morning to see tramps making their way there and back through Enton. One severe winter, around 1910 or 11, at least one didn't make it and was found frozen to death in a barn by local children. That same winter, the lake in front of Enton Hall froze and lunch was brought out from the Hall and served on the ice.

Non-conformist worship had come to Milford in the middle of the 19th century with the first little Congregational Chapel built at the junction of

Chapel Lane and Portsmouth Road in 1859 to accommodate 60 people. In 1872 a site was found in Ladycross and an iron chapel was built that remained in use for meetings until 1991. The existing church building was built in front of this in 1902. One of the foundation stones was laid by the Chairman of the Congregational Union of England and Wales. According to their son, the first couple to get married in the new church were Mr and Mrs Ernest Tracy. The church was not licensed for marriages and the couple had to get a total of 50 signatures on a special form. This they did, only to discover that the signatures should have been in duplicate and so they had to visit all the 50 people again for more signatures. The congregation at the new church grew steadily, with people walking many miles to attend its services.

Witley's doctor was Dr Booker who practised from his home, Lasham's Lea, on Lasham's Hill. His horse and cart were a familiar sight around the village for many years. Old Milfordians recall a Milford doctor doing his rounds on horseback from his practice at Wyndham Lodge in Church Road. The other side of Church Road was all fields.

After the outbreak of War in 1914, life changed dramatically. The Old Manor at Witley was used as Army Quarters. Local women enrolled with the Land Army and farmed the grounds. One of these was Violet Ford who later farmed Pleck Farm with her husband and finally ran a market garden and shop at Pleck Farmhouse on the corner of Wheeler Lane. She eventually retired a few years before she died in 1994. The shop at Crossways, now T. E. Francis, served teas to soldiers billeted at Roke House that is now Barrow Hills School.

The open heathland that characterised the whole of the Milford and Witley Commons at this time had already made it suitable for army camps and it was used as a training camp for the Imperial Yeomanry in the early years of this century.

The War Department issued special bye-laws for Witley Common in January 1915 to create a camp for the training of Canadian soldiers before they were sent to France. The Camp straddled both the London to Portsmouth and the Guildford to Haslemere Roads. It extended 1½ miles in each direction from Moushill at Milford to Bowlhead Green, with much of the common given over to the horses. It operated between early 1916 and September 1919 by which time it was a demobilisation camp. Between 30 and 50,000 troops passed through the camp, although apparently it was not known how many were there at any one time. 30,000 were said to be accommodated there during the demobilisation period.

One of the benefits of the army camp to Witley was that it was essential to extend the mains water supply that until then had been very restricted. The higher lands in Wormley and Sandhills continued to have problems with the quality of the water supplied for the next two decades.

Although primarily a camp for Canadian soldiers, it was also used as an extension of the British military facilities at Aldershot. Amongst the British soldiers who passed briefly through Witley Camp was the famous poet Wilfred Owen who joined the 5th Battalion of the Manchester Regiment as a new 2nd Lieutenant in June 1916. Amongst the poems that he is thought to have written whilst at Witley is 'A New Heaven', dedicated to an un-named soldier on active service.

The Camp was a self contained community, with its own shops and entertainment. The rows of lock up shops made from wood and corrugated iron were soon nicknamed 'Tin Town'. They were owned by local traders, mainly from Godalming, including a jeweller (Patton's) and the clothier, Pitcher's, that only ceased trading in Godalming in 1999.

There was considerable interaction, voluntary and involuntary, between the camp and the local communities. Local police records list offences committed outside the camp including rape, bigamy and larceny. Within the camp the list of offences was much longer, including drunkenness, unlawful possession of an offensive weapon, unlicensed sale of drink, indecency, larceny, shop-breaking, prostitution, and wilful murder.

The more harmonious relations included the voluntary help rendered by many Witley women in the YMCA by selling chocolate and serving teas, and the regular washing and mending of an estimated 68,000 garments. The women were transported to the camp in the horse and break owned by Mr Rollett of Wormley. There was never a shortage of volunteers. King Edward's School Band went over to the Camp to play at the Sunday morning services and to Guildford to play to the wounded there. According to School magazines of the time, the KES boys enjoyed their contact with the

Surrey Yeomanry at Milford Camp, 1903

Witley Camp, 1917

Camp, despite the long march there. The Canadian Field Artillery expressed its gratitude to the School by providing it with games gear in April 1919.

The cricket ground at Milford Heath was used by the troops as a baseball pitch. One of baseball's most famous players, Babe Ruth, played there. The heath was also used for less welcome activities and there were many complaints when experiments with gas were held. Locals were concerned about the effect of the drifting fumes on both people and plants. Mr A Chaplin of Milford remembers King George V visiting the camp. He stood on Milford Green, near what is now the Surrey Crafts Shop, to take the salute as the troops marched from the camp to Milford Station on their way to France. Lilian Wheeler, another life-long Milford resident, was at school in the village then. All the children came out of school and walked to the Green to see the King. She also remembers Edward the Prince of Wales coming to the camp, but she did not see him. Cicely Puttick was a VAD Nurse during the war, having started her working life as a secretary. She worked at the annexe to the Farnham Road Hospital in Guildford in the building that later became the County School. After the war she continued in nursing.

Frank Ashdown, who joined the choir at All Saints Church in Witley early in 1918 at the age of 9, remembered the scores of soldiers who came each week to evensong, filling the church so that the choir had to process in single file down the nave. The candles in the chandeliers were lit by the sexton, Mr Denyer. Displayed high above were the regimental colours of four Canadian Regiments which had been left in safe keeping while they went to the front in France. Two of the soldiers sang in the choir, one of whom had as his favourite hymn "Lead us, heavenly Father, lead us o'er the world's tempestuous sea". Both returned safely from France and eventually to Canada, but from one of the battalions, only nine men came back.

The choir had its full complement of fourteen boys, but its senior ranks were restricted to eight men all over 45 as the young men of the village had been taken into the armed forces. Robert Holmes, the landlord of the White Hart, and Henry Kent, the local carrier, both sang tenor with Albert Ashdown and George Edwards both singing bass. These two were head gardeners at Pinewood and Witley Manor respectively. Other choristers were Frank Young and the Enticknap brothers. Directly behind were three lady contraltos, Miss Ayling, Miss Laura Ashdown and Miss Ethel Denyer (daughter of the sexton). With them were any boy probationers.

The organist and choir master was Mr Wigan, the headmaster. The organ console was then on the opposite side of the chapel screen, so he had to turn and look back at the choir to see if the boys were behaving. Before service on Sunday mornings the boys had to gather in the big schoolroom and rehearse the chants and hymn tunes around Mr Wigan at his large American organ. When this was done to his satisfaction they would proceed across the road to the vestry. At matins and evensong they sang the set psalms for the day as well as the canticles. Stanford's setting of the Te Deum and appropriate anthems were sung at the festivals. The Reverend Sabine Baring–Gould, who wrote many well known hymns, was the uncle of the vicar's wife and when he visited his niece he was a popular speaker with the children at Sunday School.

Discontent at the camp started as soon as the Armistice was declared, with riots on November 11th causing damage to shops in Tin Town estimated at £8,757-7-11½. Many threats were made against the shopkeepers that the shops would be looted and destroyed during the Christmas week of 1918, but trouble was held off until the February and June of 1919. The Canadians, like their British counterparts, felt that the demobilisation system was unfair and wanted to get home without further delay. The arrest and confinement of some men by the Canadian Military Police caused a riotous assembly of soldiers in the camp on the night of the 9th and morning of the 10th February. The soldiers were forcibly freed from custody and the men then turned against the Officers' Quarters, which were wrecked, their canteen looted and all the drink stolen. The Tin Town shops were then ruined. Action to claim compensation was taken by several shop owners against the Canadian Military Authorities but all failed. The claimants turned to Surrey County Council, being the Police Authority for the area, but they too denied responsibility claiming that the area was under military control. The buck passed to and fro until final settlement was adjudicated in the Court of Appeal in February 1923 in a test case of Pitchers against the County Council. The three judges all agreed that the land had never been excluded from the civil police area, with the military barracks and the camp both under civil law.

Further rioting and trouble in June 1919 resulted in several soldiers being tried and punished by Courts Martial on various charges including mutiny. Mrs Talman remembers a huge explosion at the camp from all the ammunition being destroyed. From her bedroom in Step Cottage she could see the flames shooting high in the sky. The explosion was large enough to make some of the properties in the area move slightly. The records of the riots do not include mention of this action, although Mrs Talman's understanding was that it was the presence of all this ammunition that was delaying the return of the troops: the Camp could not be cleared until provision had been made for it and this was taking too long for the soldiers' liking.

At the end of the war, the Canadian government gave Witley Women one of the camp huts in appreciation of their help. The hut, set on the school drill ground, became the centre of activities for village women of all ages. There were social evenings, dances, athletics, a girls' club and a choir. The Women's Hut joined the Village Institute that had been built in 1883 (now the British Legion), the School and the Church as centres of village life. Further down the road at Crossways, the Working Men's Club was started in another army hut and this also accommodated the Scout troop. The Women's Hut eventually began to be used more by youth groups: the first youth club was held there before moving to Lasham's Barn when the Scouts took over the hut. Another of the huts was erected by Mr Ernie Rothwell, the Milford butcher and milkman, in Church Road, as the village's first

The White Hart ca 1914, before extension

Community Assembly Rooms. The land was donated by the wife of Archdeacon Potter of Rake Manor. Other huts were removed from the camp and turned into houses: several of these can still be seen around the villages although some have now been clad with other finishes.

The last year of the war was also the time of a severe 'flu epidemic that killed so many that the sexton had to dig graves by lamplight and moonlight to cope with the demand. According to Leslie Bonner, who was then living at Enton, the sexton emerged one night from a newly dug grave just as someone he knew was going home from the 'White Hart' along the footpath through the churchyard. The sexton's cheery greeting caused the man to flee in fright!

Chapter 2

The Large Houses and Estates

The big houses around these villages provided considerable employment for local people and shaped both social structures and the appearance of the countryside. There were several such houses around. Wildcroft House was notable for its large stable of 90 donkeys. The stables fronted Gasden Lane, on much of the land that is now occupied by the houses along Wildcroft Wood. The last groom died in 1998. His funeral was marked by a horse drawn hearse travelling through many of the side roads in Witley and Milford, taking him on a familiar journey for the last time.

The Enton estate originally had two houses, Great Enton and Enton Lodge, but in the 1880s the larger Enton Hall was built. A leaden box was placed under a foundation stone, containing a copy of the London Times of the day and every coin of the realm. The estate was owned at the time and into this century by Mr John Eastwood, an old fashioned autocrat, but regarded as a kindly man. During his time, Sweetwater Lake was created by building a brick dam across a small stream which came from the commons behind the estate. There were thirty five tied cottages on the estate for the woodmen, gamekeepers, estate workers and farm hands. They were well built brick cottages, with large gardens so that the estate men could all keep pigs for their own use and grow their own vegetables. The estate had its own qualified nurse who looked after the women during child-birth and the children when they were ill.

Mrs Smithers of Church Lane, Witley, came to work as the assistant cook at Enton Hall in November 1926, one of 13 servants at the Hall. By then the Hall was owned by Major and Mrs Chichester. On church festivals like Easter, there was communion at church at 6 and 7 a.m. so that all local servants could attend before starting their domestic duties. Mrs Smithers worked at the Hall for 8 years, leaving to get married. She had been offered a house on the estate, but was not able to look at it until after she had handed in her notice as it was still occupied. When she and her husband-to-be saw it, they could not accept it as it was in a poor state of repair, and still with earth floors throughout. Expectations had changed with time, and they deemed it unsuitable for their new furniture.

Rake Manor was extensively altered during the last part of the 19th century, first by Ralph Nevill, FSA, and then by Edwin Lutyens during which time it was first designated as 'Rake Manor'. Gertrude Jekyll and Lutyens were both friends of the tenant, Mrs Cavan Irving, who held the property between 1885 and 1906 and both were used to remodel parts of the house and grounds. In 1906, the property was sold to Rev. Beresford Potter, Archdeacon in Cyprus between 1901 and 1928, and his wife, Sarah, who was the granddaughter of one of the founders of the Lea and Perrins Sauce company. Their tenure of Rake saw further substantial building works under the direction of the well known arts and crafts architect, Baillie Scott. He was also employed along with Raymond Carcy by the next owners in the 1930s for the final stages of alterations to the house.

Rake Manor ca 1915

Witley Park was united into one estate by Mr Whitaker Wright who bought the Le Ley Estate from Park Lane to Thursley Common and Witley from J. W. Stone JP in 1885 for an estimated £150,000, and the Witley Park end between Park Lane and Hindhead from the Earl of Derby in 1890. Whitaker Wright employed Paxton Watson as the architect for a new main house, stables and lodges, demolishing the old Lea Park House but retaining its name. The project took over seven years to complete and included the building of three lakes, each dug by hand and traction engine, with cobbled banks to make them secure. Edwin Lutyens was commissioned to build a swimming hut, a boat house, a bridge at the end of Spring Lake and the Well House. Brunel was commissioned to design the tunnel that goes to the false island in Thursley Lake.

The reconstruction of Witley Park cost over £1.25 million. The embellishments he made to the house were famous. In the large kitchens there was a fountain at either end to help cool the air. The drawing room ceiling had a cornice of solid gold. In the grounds there was a smoking room underneath the centre of an ornamental lake. The walls and ceiling of the smoking room were plate glass. There were two access routes to this room; one was from a tunnel from the bank of the lake and the other way was by rowing out to a small temple which was on pillars in the centre of the lake. Another small temple stood beside the lake, with a well in the centre of it and a pool of crystal clear water. In the bottom of the well was a white marble bust of a lady. Legend had it that anyone trying to touch this bust would die suddenly.

A workman repairing and cleaning the temple declared he did not believe the legend and put his hand in the water, trying to touch the lady's head. The well was deeper than he thought so he did not succeed, but after dinner that night he dropped dead. The house and a large part of the park was surrounded by a ten foot high wall, extending over seven miles. In the winter, Whitaker Wright would often have a length of the wall broken down to give the local men work. Not surprisingly, he was very popular and well respected locally.

He did not enjoy the fruits of his labours for long: in 1903 Whitaker Wright was the subject of a fraud enquiry. He was charged with creating two fictitious mining companies in South Africa and selling the shares on the London Stock Exchange. He hid in the Ice House, a subterranean storage room at the Park, for two weeks before fleeing to New York. He was arrested and extradited to the UK, standing trial in 1905. Witley Park was taken into receivership. Before his trial he told Mr Eastwood that if sentenced, he would never serve his term. After a sentence of seven years was passed on him at the Old Bailey, he was taken to the cells below. He asked if he could smoke a cigar. The cigar had been specially prepared with a cyanide pellet

Lea Park, 1906

Drawing room in Lea Park with ornate gold cornice

Grounds of Lea Park, with temple in ornamental lake

in the mouthpiece so he died instantly. Hundreds of people came to his funeral at Witley Church with everyone at the graveside being given a bunch of violets and asked to drop them into his grave. After the funeral was over, his grave was completely full of violets. On his tombstone is inscribed 'He loved the poor'.

During the first world war, so many Canadian soldiers came to see Whitaker Wright's grave that his widow had the inscription altered to JAMES W. WRIGHT. After the war, Mrs Whitaker Wright used to put money on his memorial, much to the delight of the children who raced out of the school opposite to retrieve it. Eventually the vicar gently asked her not to do it any more.

In 1905, Lord Pirrie, a director of the White Star Shipping Line that later operated the 'Titanic', bought the Estate. His star insignia is still much in evidence on many gates around the park. Lord Pirrie is best remembered as the benefactor who gave the land for the cricket ground at Brook, and had the Pirrie Hall built next to it. The Estate was sold in 1927 to Sir John Leigh, who changed the name to Witley Park, probably to avoid confusion with his own name. The Estate was requisitioned by the Government during the second world war, and sold in May 1952. On 11th October, 1952 a fire started in the Great Ballroom that gutted the house. A new house was built in 1962 by the Bentall family, which is now the private house of the present owner who acquired the 1500 acre estate in 1981. The Estate is still privately run, and since 1991 has operated as a conference centre.

Chapter 3

Brook and Sandhills

Like other parts of the Parish, Brook and Sandhills are now home to many commuters who know little of life here as it used to be. However, some remain who continue the earlier tradition when labourers rather than moneyed people filled most of the houses. Sandhills' narrow, twisting roads have helped preserve much of its old world charm, and many of its senior citizens have delighted in sharing their memories.

The Brook village hall (the Pirrie Hall), was erected in 1923 by Lord Pirrie. It was for the use of the inhabitants of Brook and Sandhills generally but particularly for the Women's Institute, who, at the outset, provided the hall with new Lloyd Loom chairs. The WI, originally called Sandhills and Brook WI, had been formed in 1919 and first met at Institute Cottage. Through stalwarts such as Joey Makovski and Miss Marouski, who were members for over 60 years, the WI was at the heart of many village activities. For example, in 1946 they started old-time dancing, which - in 1947 - led to the formation of a dancing club with over a hundred members up to its closure in the late 1960s. With up to about 60 members in its heyday, the WI was very successful, but in 1998, when membership fell to just 17, it was forced to close.

Other regular activities which used to take place at the Pirrie Hall included billiards. Indeed, what is now the nursery was actually a purpose-made billiards room. The bowling green and club have gone too, but tennis and table tennis have flourished in their place, perhaps more in tune with the gradual change in local society. As Len Cole recalls: 'We used to have all sorts of entertainments, but along came the television and the combustion engine and it was all gone'.

The hall also used to have a youth club, attracting some seventy children from quite a wide area every Friday night. The annual Christmas party survived for rather longer, into the late 1980s. Those who attended now look back on these with great affection. Fred Ashwell recalls how, in predecimal days 'just half-a-crown would be enough to buy a good present for each child. All the kids used to gather outside, shouting "We want Father Christmas", and when he rang his bell all hell broke loose as they ran in. They also each received an orange from the cricket club.'

When the Pirrie Hall was built a new cricket green was established at its front, the sport previously having been played behind Redlands, at Sandhills; but the original site continued to be called the cricket field until only a few years ago. Len Cole of Gasden Copse, who was team treasurer in the early 1950s, recalls: 'The standard was very good and it was real village cricket then, with all local players, but nowadays hardly any of the players live here.'

Pirrie Hall, 1999

Today the cricket is highly competitive and some of Brook's teams have been very successful. Any dog walker venturing onto the hallowed turf is likely to be shot on sight! Fred Ashwell of Sandhills, long-time caretaker of the Pirrie Hall, is one of many people who preferred the much more informal early days: 'Every Sunday evening we'd go down and barrack the cricketers - it was the done thing. And as soon as the cricket finished it was over the road to the Dog - that was your Sunday evening.'

Among the people who used to bring celebrity teams to play at Brook was the dilettante actor and artist W. Graham Robertson. Len Cole still vividly remembers the day when the famous artist Augustus John was among Robertson's guests: 'He was somewhat rotund and as he bent down to pick up the ball on the boundary his flannels dropped like a stone. Then he was in a real quandary and didn't know what to do first - pick up his trousers to save embarrassment or return the ball to save runs. In the end discretion had the better part of valour.'

Graham Robertson was one of many well-known artists and writers who have been attracted to the beautiful countryside of south-west Surrey - especially Sandhills - since Victorian times. In 1889 this wealthy 21-year-old bought the Sandhills house confusingly called 'Sandhills' and over many years became established as the local 'squire', also owning most of the near-by cottages.

The eccentric Robertson died at 'Sandhills' in 1949 and his home farm later became what is now known as 'The Donkey Farm', the well-known sanctuary established and run by the Lockwoods to this present day. Both his home and studio/rehearsal room along Sandhills Lane had been visited by many leading actors and artists of the day, ranging from Henry Irving to Burne-Jones, from John Gielgud to Ellen Terry, whose portrait he painted and hung in the studio for many years. In 1900, Ellen Terry wrote to Robertson from America, saying: 'Some of my very peacefullest and happiest hours have been at your cottage.'

Apart from writing books and painting pictures, Robertson also wrote and produced the Chiddingfold and Guildford Pageant Plays. He founded the Chiddingfold Players Amateur Dramatic Group who toured local villages with their productions. His book of reminiscences, 'Time Was', published in 1931, includes a chapter called 'Back To The Land', which is all about his coming to Sandhills. Robertson described the Sandhills of the 1880s as '...a most unsophisticated little village and might have been many hundred miles from town...really rustic and unspoilt...ancient legends and beliefs still lingered and the older villagers were still the heirs of the ages and wise with the wisdom of the years.'

With its excellent acoustics, Robertson's lovely old studio was a fitting place for the WI to hold choir practice. It has remained as a focus for art up to this present day, continuing to foster some promising young talent. For many years it was the studio of the late, internationally acclaimed artist Stefan Knapp, a Polish emigré.

Many of Knapp's sculptures and paintings adorn gardens, skyscrapers and other large buildings around the world, providing sharp contrast to the very traditional work of earlier Sandhills' artists, such as the very successful Myles Birket Foster. While Knapp pioneered the use of enamels on metal, Foster executed fine watercolours of local scenes and people. In 1875 he helped re-paint the sign of the White Hart, at Witley: that original sign is now in the Victoria and Albert Museum.

However, there is little doubt that the most famous artist who ever lived in our area was Helen Allingham, originally a pupil of Birket Foster. Known chiefly for her idyllic scenes of country cottages with roses round the door and rustics in the garden, she was largely inspired by the eight years she spent at Sandhills. Ironically, she lived in the largest house in Sandhills, the place called 'Sandhills' which she sold to Graham Robertson in 1889. She moved to Bloomsbury so that her children could be better educated, yet died in this parish, in 1926, when she returned to walk the hills and paint once more with Graham Robertson and other local friends.

Helen Allingham and her artist husband, William, were among the first people to show great concern for our rich architectural heritage. Among the people they pressed to take more care of their buildings and pathways was Lord Derby, the largely absentee landlord who owned Witley Park. She painted innumerable watercolours of the cottages and views in and around Brook and Sandhills, some of which are superficially unchanged to this day. However, in her desire to idealise she often distorted the truth and in her pictures 're-thatched' cottages which had long been tiled. In fact, she subsequently admitted that by 1880 there was only one thatched house left in her part of Surrey, a cottage in Wormley Wood.

In this area, Helen Allingham befriended other famous artists and writers, not least the Poet Laureate Lord Tennyson, who lived at Blackdown and loved to walk the inspirational local hills. Another visitor was old friend Kate Greenaway, who became famous for her children's books and often came down to Witley to stay with her publisher, Edmund Evans.

Among Allingham's watercolours is a splendid view of Master Hardy's cottage, in the foreground of which are the sandhills which gave the village its name. Sadly, the sand martins nesting in burrows within the sand cliff face are now a rare sight. John Hardy was Allingham's gardener and she 'acquired' him along with his cottage next door when she took over the lease. Since then the name of Hardy has been synonymous with Brook, notably through local builders Alan and Roy Hardy, the grandsons of John the gardener. Alan, even when not living nearby, has been the backbone of the cricket club for over half a century, captaining innumerable matches and doing so much to cultivate much of today's talent. Roy still lives with his family in one of the cottages.

Another Hardy linked with Allingham was Rhoda, whom the artist painted as a young girl, before she became Mrs Burgess and the landlady of the Dog and Pheasant. In those days the pub had the two traditional, separate bars and was weather-boarded. Postcards from the first two decades of this century also show that there used to be a large cottage to the left of the pub front, where the garden is now situated, and right across the front was the name Lascelles, presumably the brewer. Another old view shows a horse grazing on the ground across the road from the pub. Adjacent to the pub was a forge. The Reynolds still sometimes uncover horse-shoes when they dig the bottom of their garden opposite, at Brook Cottage.

Like so many country pubs, in the old days the Dog and Pheasant had very few landlords. The very popular 'Jug' (Doug) Keary and his son John were there for about a quarter of a century up to the early 1990s, and before them the Platts called time. Apparently Mr Platt was a great practical joker, who glued coins to the counter to fox unsuspecting customers. He also had an imitation spider on a string, which he would lower onto the shoulders of young ladies when they stood at the bar. Furthermore, he had a notice on the lawn stating: 'This way to the water otter'. It led to a doorway on the wall separating Brook Park, but anyone opening it would have been very disappointed to find nothing other than a false door and frame nailed to the wall, and that the so-called water otter was an old black kettle on a chain!

Among the pub's great character customers in those days was Lew Edwards, the recently retired 87-year-old coppicer whose father was labourer for Lord Pirrie and helped to build the fine stone wall which still stands around Witley Park. From the age of sixteen up to World War 2, Lew played cricket for Brook, as well as football for Brook and Grayswood United. He recalls: 'I played nearly every Saturday and Sunday, in the second eleven, but I haven't taken hold of a bat since the war. I only went for the social side really - a good ol' sing-song in the pub after. It was good in the pub then; if they were local people you knew 'em. I remember goin' down the Dog and Pheasant on my eighteenth birthday and got chucked out the same night. And it weren't my fault either. They were good ol' days. If you 'ad 'alf-a-crown in yer pocket you could face the evenin' comfortable. But many a time I went with a shillin'. You'd buy the first brown for 4½d (we'd buy a pint and split it if we could, as it was cheaper at 7d), get on the ol' dartboard, and if you won a couple of games you was all right as your beer was paid for. But if you lost you 'ad to sit in the corner, quiet like.'

The dartboard has long since disappeared from the pub, as more space has been needed for the ever-growing number of people eating out. The quoits have gone, too, including the bed which used to be outside 'The Willows'. Once it was an extremely popular game, with another pitch not far away at Milford Green. Fred Ashwell recalls how 'Perc Hardy used to walk all the way from Sandhills to the 'Parrot' at Shalford to play quoits'. Sandhills, too, once had a pub - the Sebastopol in Sebastopol Lane. Now locals must use either the Dog and Pheasant or walk to the very end of Church Lane, to the White Hart, the pub said to have the oldest continuous licence in Britain, dating back to the 14th Century.

One of the few local places offering employment apart from local farms and estates was Brook brickyard, which continued into the late 1940s. On behalf of the builders Milton's, this was run by the two Mercer brothers and their father, who had a few others to help them and lived at the ancient Goose Cottage. For decades Tom Mercer was known as one of the great characters of the pub. Fred Ashwell recalls: 'When they fired the brickyard kiln up they couldn't leave it, but it was real thirsty work so they'd send someone up the Dog to keep 'em supplied.'

Fred Ashwell came to Sandhills in 1949, when he married local girl Dorothy Bookham. Before that he'd thought nothing of walking all the way over from Hambledon in the snow, for a spot of courting. But then most country folk were used to walking long distances, which is just as well because Sandhills has never had much of a bus service. Being on a main road, Brook was well served by buses, which ran as frequently as two-hourly in the 1950s, but for most of the time Sandhills was left out on a limb. It did have buses for a few years, but they came through only once or twice a week! In 1999, a community bus service was started by the Parish Council that includes both Brook and Sandhills on its weekly run to Godalming. Fortunately, Witley station is on the main Portsmouth to Waterloo line and only a short walk away for commuters from Brook and Sandhills.

As it was not a major stagecoach or main mail route, the A286 remained unspoilt during the early 20th Century. It was metalled in the late 1920s or early 1930s but some of the bends and dips were not removed until much later. For example, the old road used to run where the layby now is between Brook Rocks and the Dog and Pheasant, and the dip in the A286 near Wareham House - between Brook Crossroads and Upper Birtley - used to be much steeper, proving a great obstacle in snow or ice. Within living memory, Brook and Sandhills do not appear to have had any resident policemen, but Joey Makovski remembers that 'the bobby from Witley had to be at the telephone box at a certain time each day. Others were based at Thursley and Milford, but rarely called upon as there was so little crime.'

Brook's last post office and shop was run by the Wellands, next to the Dog and Pheasant in part of the house known as The Gables. The same family owned the ancient Sister Cottage next door, where there used to be a slaughter house serving the adjacent butcher, in a green timber building where the drive is now.

As in other small rural communities, some shops were little more than an extension or adaptation of someone's cottage. For example, the Ashwells remember: 'In Conker Cottage, behind the telephone box at Sandhills, there used to be an old boy who sold tobacco and cigarettes. And in one of the pair of cottages opposite Brook Dene there was an old lady who sold tea, coffee, sugar and sweets, and she made her own sweet bags out of paper.'

With few private cars around there was more reliance on food deliveries, even in days when families generally were more self-sufficient. Lew Edwards remembers that when his family lived at Roundles Cottage, which was Creedhole Farm, 'the grocer used to come round once a week, on a Friday, from Milford Supply Store. Also, Summers the baker came out three times a week, on his horse and cart from Grayswood.' Dorothy

Ashwell recalls that 'when Mr Hanscombe used to come out on his bike with your groceries, from the International Stores, he'd take your order for the following week. And Winston used to come out with fish from Chiddingfold. If you wanted a bit "for the cat" he'd always oblige and give you six pennies' worth, and when he went to one of the big houses he'd put sixpence on their bill to make up.'

'Then there was Jockey Hammond, who used to come round on his bike with a basket on the front. He brought bootlaces, elastic, buttons and so on; and if you had a rabbit skin he'd give you sixpence for it. He was one of those fairground people from Hambledon and he called in winter when there were no fairs on.'

Len Cole remembers that Fulbrook's (later Hammond's) delivered bread from Milford on every other day (a service that continued until Hammond's closed in 1998). Also, his own father delivered milk on a bike, with a large can and ladle, but he had to abandon this at the beginning of the war, following the establishment of the Milk Marketing Board. In those days the Coles lived on a small farm on the edge of Witley Common. The old house has long gone but Len clearly remembers his life there: 'My boyhood was dominated by cattle. Father started with nothing after the first war and we didn't have enough grazing, so we used to run the cows on Witley Common, where we also cut bracken for their bedding. It was my job to look after them - after school each day and every Sunday morning. Then they could come back home on their own - across the main road! Imagine what would happen now if they tried that with all the traffic tearing past!'

Despite this, Len also found time to earn a bit of pocket money by going beating on shoots at Witley Park: 'We earned the princely sum of 5 shillings each plus all we could eat. They'd come round with a whole cheese and great chunks of bread. There was beer too, and when us lads asked if there was any lemonade we were told "It's beer or nothing"! In those days there was so much game about, with pheasants and rabbits runnin' all round your feet. For us in the beating line the object was to get near the wall so that you could sling a bird over and pick it up when you went. This was just pre-war, when Bob Curtis was the headkeeper. In those days rabbit was the staple diet and any time you wanted one you'd just go up to old Clem's hut up in the woods and pick one out.' Lew Edwards recalls that back in 1936 there were so many rabbits on the Witley Park estate, despite there being 28 gamekeepers there, the owner - Sir John Leigh - imported buzzards from Scotland in 1939 in an attempt to control them. At first they were kept in cages to acclimatise them, 'but when the war came there was no labour to look after them so they all had to be released.' Today they are an increasingly common sight in the area.

Like most country lads, Fred Ashwell too was not averse to a spot of poaching: 'I used to catch fish in Witley Park lake, using a bamboo for a rod'. He also joined in with the usual schoolboy pranks: 'Once we found a huge lorry tyre out on the A3 and we rolled it all the way back to Lake Cottages, where we lived at the time. We went to the top of the hill on the common and let it go. Down and down it bounced until it hit the double oak doors of Lake Lodge, where the head gardener lived. Unfortunately, his wife had just been out and done her step all nice and this tyre was full of soil and water, so when it toppled over there it made an awful mess.'

As far as we know, the only house deliberately demolished in Brook and Sandhills this century is the cottage that used to stand next to the Dog and Pheasant; and with ever stricter planning controls it is not surprising that very few completely new homes have been built. Only four have gone up in Sandhills while Brook has had but a few council houses and the very recent development at Brook Farm, next to the pub. This is partly due to the vigilance and concern of villagers, who rallied round to defeat a proposed development of the old brickyard site in the mid-1990s.

Len Cole recalls: 'Where there is one house with one family in now there used to be two, three or four families all squashed in.' Typical of rural areas, they had few 'mod cons' too. For example, Fred Ashwell remembers: 'The ol' donkey cart man used to come round on a Friday night, with his bucket to empty your toilet; oh yes! And many a New Year's night we used to ask him in for a drink.' That said, many houses in the area are still on private drainage and there is still no mains gas in and around Brook and Sandhills. Furthermore, a few houses, such as those at Upper Birtley, are still on a private water supply, though this is treasured by most residents for its purity and softness. Surprisingly, although nearby Godalming was the first town in Britain to have a public electricity supply, some houses in Brook and Sandhills did not get theirs until the mid-1950s.

Luckily, during World War 2 enemy action caused little damage in this area. Joey Makovski recalls: 'One day we heard these bangs and thought we'd better take a look. My fellow air raid warden was one of the Witley gardeners - Birtles - and we discovered that a string of bombs had been dropped across the park. Birtles said "Look at all these leaves everywhere - people will think I've not been doing my job", but I said don't be silly - they're all petals - one of the bombs had fallen in the dahlia bed! Fortunately, they'd just missed the stables, where three or four hundred Canadian troops were billeted. The total death toll was just two rabbits and two fish! Neither was anyone killed at Birtley when one of the cottages was hit.'

The Ashwells recall that a doodlebug landed on the garage of the Waller's cottage in Church Lane, but nobody was hurt. Also, King Edward's School was nearly hit. When the bomber crashed one of the Germans bailed out and was taken to the Red Cross centre at the Chichester Hall.

During the war a number of larger local houses were occupied by the Army, including Kingwood, Pinewood and Broomhill. At one time Kingwood had Italian prisoners there and they appear to have been quite happy, being allowed to go down to the woods to collect willow for basket-making. Ex-fighter pilot and one-time Lord Mayor of London, the late Sir George Wilkinson, established a craft centre at Kingwood, making toys, furniture and pottery. Mr David Real, who was the potter there, went on to start the Grayshott Pottery. Sir George Wilkinson also bought land from the old Witley Park estate, on the eastern side of the A286 at Upper and Lower Birtley. Lord Pirrie's monogram can still be seen on some of the old iron gates there.

Great community spirit remains in Brook and Sandhills, chiefly centred around those bastions of English country life - the pub, cricket and the village hall. Brook Fete is still the highlight of the year, going from strength to strength with Lady Carole Brown as the enthusiastic and generous president of the committee. John and Suzzi Rachkind, with a host of hardworking volunteers, manage to blend the best of old and new. The emphasis is still on good old-fashioned fun, but there is also an important willingness to look to the future seeking out new ideas which will continue to attract the younger generation. The support of all is vital for the Pirrie Hall to be expanded and remain at the heart of the local community into the next millennium.

Chapter 4

Daily Life until 1939

Many of what are now residential streets in Witley and Milford were farm land, market gardens, nurseries and fields between the wars. In Witley, there were fields and market gardens between Roke Lane and Wheeler Lane and several outlets for fresh vegetables in the village. The land that is now occupied by the Chandler School was, until 1974, Eliot's market garden with long rows of runner beans supplying Covent Garden. No-one in the village bothered to grow their own beans as you could buy a large bag there for 3d. Sunnydown was renowned within the area as a carrot nursery and Rawlinson's specialised in tomatoes and cucumbers. The road Merry Acres, off Cramhurst Lane, was another farm selling vegetables until the early 70s. Part of Willowmead and Willowcroft down to 'Clare Lodge' was Scott's, a world famous carnation nursery. 'Clare Lodge' was then called 'The Gables' and its land extended down through a croquet lawn to what is now Bannister Close. The property belonged to an electrical engineer who worked in the Gold Coast (Ghana), and who built his own generator for electricity at 'The Gables'. Middlemarch was, until 1914, a famous rose nursery run by a German who developed and had named after him the rose 'Papa Meilland'. He was interned during the war and never returned to Witley. The Old Manor near the Star sold milk from its own herd until Stovold's Dairy from Eashing started a delivery service. The Fords too were dairy farmers, with Violet doing the early morning milking, helped by the Mullard children. The cows were kept in a field behind the Mullard's house, and the children learnt the technique of milking. Mr Ford sold the milk from a can, measured into his customers' jugs. The milk cans were slung from the handlebars of his bike.

In Milford, most of the land around the Crossroads was occupied by Hurst Farm. The dairy was where the public car park is now. Pigs were slaughtered by shooting them in the farmyard: local children gathering round to watch were warned not to stand behind the animal as the bullet would go right through. The carcasses were taken over the road to Rothwell's butchers shop, but the offal and rubbish were dumped in Chapel Lane, attracting all the local dogs. The dogs and the smell both upset the residents.

Other daily needs could also be met within the confines of the villages, although even then some people preferred to go into Godalming for their shopping. Each part of both villages had some stores, with a baker at both Wormley and Culmer and shops in Milford at the Crossroads, New Road and Moushill. In Witley on Lashams Hill there was a butcher, Mr Rothwell, on the corner of Milton's Yard, a branch of Lloyds Bank and the general grocer Forrest Stores run by Mr Sanders next to the Post Office on the corner of Northfields. The original post office occupied the premises that later became the bank. All these retail outlets have been progressively lost and the Sun Inn itself closed between the wars. It was not a full inn, only a beer house as it had no licence for wines and spirits. There was another branch of Lloyds Bank next to the original post office at Milford Crossroads: the horse emblem can still be seen etched above the door. Forrest Stores, which was a regional grocery chain, took over the neighbouring premises when Milford Post Office moved to its present site.

Sun Inn and Bank, Witley, ca.1924

In Witley the Co-Op was in Chester House. The newsagency was run by the Stent family during the 1930s. Their son and a nephew delivered papers around a large part of the surrounding area. Another market garden,

George King's, occupied the land behind Crossways Cottage where the Kings lived. He also owned the land where the houses 'Nutfield' and 'Apple Trees' stand near the War Memorial. On the opposite corner of Mill Lane was a general store, Bartlett's, where almost everything could be found. The row of cottages opposite the Co-Op housed a bike shop on the corner of the lane to Enton, a sweet shop cum general store owned by Miss Muggeridge and a butcher, originally Wardley's. The bike shop was the first to go but the other shops survived until the mid 1980s. The other corner cottage has always been a house. A cobbler, Sid Hardy, operated from next door to 'Donkey Door' in the row of Tudor Cottages on Lasham's Hill between the wars. He had lost a leg in the first war, and used one crutch. After his death, the business was taken over first by the Landins and then by the Herringtons, but most people only mention Peter White who worked for both of them.

In later years Mr Wooton had a little shop at 'Donkey Door' from which he sold electrical goods and charged the small accumulators used by people in their wireless sets. The importance of horses to village life was evident in that there was a harness maker, Austin Denyer, in New Road, Milford, and a farrier in what was then an open yard in front of the group of four cottages opposite the Hut in Church Lane, Witley.

Another Denyer, Steve, ran a Corn Merchant's at the Haslemere Road end of New Road. The village cobbler operated from a tin hut where the Crossroads Surgery now stands. Milford was well supplied with garages, with one in Church Road, one on the corner of Cherry Tree and the old Portsmouth Roads and a third, Smallpieces, on the Portsmouth Road opposite the end of New Road. Smallpieces provided the open top, hooded coach that took the Sunday School children on their annual outing to Frensham Ponds, a highlight of the year. Warners coach company was based next to the White Lion pub, where its car park now is.

The shop next to the Post Office, now the NFU offices, was a sweet shop and tobacconist. There was little money around, but the local children saved what they could earn to spend there at Christmas. One way of earning a few pence was from carol singing, but for the rest of the year the children went around scooping up the horse droppings and selling it. One reliable customer was Lily Hill who lived first in Chapel Lane and then in Church Road. She was popular with the children as she made them jam tarts in return for their collecting efforts. Lily Hill was well known to everyone in the village as she played the organ in church and at the hospital.

The pound in Milford for stray animals was situated where Secrett's Farm Shop car park is now. It was quite a high structure but the children used to like going around the top of it, feeding the horses. Mr F. Sparks, who lived in Chapel Lane from 1916 to 1938, remembers hearing the horses galloping around the village most nights. He does not know how they got out so often, especially as there was £1 to pay to get them back again after they had been rounded up.

Mrs Talman lived in one of the converted workhouse cottages opposite the Star in Witley, extensively re-fitted by her painter and decorator husband. They moved there in 1927, at which time he was the only decorator in the village, and got most of the local business. Before her marriage, Mrs Talman was a lady's maid in Chiddingfold. She walked to work every day, and it was there that she met her husband. The Wheeler Street in front of her cottage changed beyond all recognition during her life in the village. She remembers it first as a narrow gravel road, only just wide enough for the horse and carts. There would have been one or two regular road men, breaking up stone at the roadside and filling the holes which developed in the untarred surfaces. It was unlit until 1914 when acetylene lamps were installed, but electricity was not generally available in the village until 1932.

Mr Percy Childs of Milford was born in Oxted Green in 1918 in the house his grandfather had occupied when it was first built and where his father continued to live after his marriage in 1914. Oxted Green was a sandy track with the River Ock running across it at the Petworth Road end. The river ran through Harbour Copse. The copse was where the day centre and adjoining field are now. It was cleared of trees towards the end of the 1920s with horses dragging out the timber and carting it away on low drays.

Percy was the first customer at Mrs Newman's shop which opened in Oxted Green during the 1920s. She had tables with dishes of sweets on, and every anniversary of the shop's opening, she gave him some of the sweets. She later expanded the shop to sell paraffin and groceries. Further up the road was a laundry.

River Ock crossing Oxted Green ca 1917

Oxted Green, ca 1937. Dick Harvey is the middle cyclist

At the beginning of the 1930s, the gas company offered to lay gas along the road. There was wide acceptance of the chance for gas lamps to light the houses. Within months of the installation, the electricity company came along, offering to connect the houses to electricity. Having just paid out for gas, there were few house-owners or landlords who could take up the offer, and it was many years before his house was connected. Houses were connected individually rather than en bloc.

Miss Mullard, whose family has lived in Witley for generations, remembers electricity coming along the main road to Witley houses. Each household was allowed to have four lights installed free of charge. Very few could afford to have more. The Talmans were pleased to have the electric lighting as Mr Talman was very tall and regularly used to break the old gas mantles by knocking into them, plunging the house into darkness until he could get a replacement the next day in Godalming. Mabel Butler, who was nanny to the Portman family at Hangerfield in Church Lane from 1927, recalls a generator making their electricity. After she married in 1937, she and her husband moved into what is now Culmerdale Farm but was then Culmer Cottage. It had been the gamekeeper's cottage on the Pirrie estate until it was part of a 3 acre lot bought by Major Portman. Electricity did not reach Culmer until two or three years after the war.

The many complaints about overflowing cesspools in various parts of both villages finally achieved limited results just before the war. The Chapel Lane area of Milford was especially notorious. The night soil cart used to run regularly down Wormley Hill, and there was constant pressure to have the zone for cesspit emptying extended. A mains sewerage system was provided. Although those who paid for connection to the new drainage system thought it expensive at the time, they were grateful to be spared the inevitable problems that arose from cesspits, especially if these were shared. The cesspits were only for sink waste: there were no water closets, only earth privies in a garden shed, sometimes attached to the house, sometimes down the garden.

Such services were restricted to properties along the main road in Witley as both mains water and sewerage did not reach the properties in, for example, Church Lane, until after the war. Although mains water is now universal, a mains sewer supply is not. Mrs Smithers, who moved into Old Barn Cottage in 1938 recalls the excellent taste of the water from the well shared between her cottage and the neighbouring Rose Cottage. Another well supplied Step Cottages, and one supplied Stone Cottages. The well at Well Villa near the British Legion which was also fed off the same stream is still checked regularly by the water company to assess water levels. The well at Rose Cottage is at least 40 feet deep and had a windlass that wound up two buckets at a time. Every Monday, 16 buckets had to be pulled up to fill the copper for the weekly wash. Further down the hill, the water was less tasty, and that drawn from wells in Wheeler Lane had to be boiled. Most houses had a pump in the scullery, but the house between the Red Lion in Milford and Forrest Stores had its well in the kitchen. This house was lived in by the actor Cecil Parker.

Open top buses started running an hourly service through Witley in 1921 and up to the beginning of the war, there was always the theatre bus which got back to Witley just after midnight on a Saturday night. The road was very narrow: it was widened from the bottom of Church Lane to the bottom of Culmer Hill around 1930, with a bank and hedge dug out to make the footpath and grass as it is now. Further widening at the bottom of the village between Wheeler Lane and Roke Lane did not occur until about 30 years later.

The villages were essentially self sufficient communities, with plenty of local employment available. Building materials came either from Milton's Yard or Mullard's Yard. Jack Milton lived in Hillbrow, adjacent to his yard and employed up to 200 people. His firm built many of the properties in Witley and Wormley. The Milford builder was Rainsford's, whose yard was where Milford Glass is now. Bricks were made at Wareham Hill in Brook; timber could come from Keen's on Haslemere Road or the Wharf at Godalming to the sawmill in Roke Lane by Eastfields. Luck's the Milford plumber was well established. Near to where the Chichester Hall now stands, children going home from school often stood to watch Mr Mitchell, the stone mason, chipping away or smoothing some marble gravestone prior to its being erected in the churchyard. Later on, this trade was carried on by Mr E Mullard. Mr Mullard was also a bell ringer and rang the last knell to be sounded from Witley belfry, when King George V died. After Mr Mullard retired, his workshops were dismantled and moved to the Weald and Downland Museum at Singleton, W. Sussex where they can still be seen.

Coal was a necessity in all households, and it was hawked round in hundredweight sacks on horse-drawn flat drays. It came from the railway stations at Milford or Witley, for then they had goods-sidings, and could receive ten-ton trucks from the mines. A daily goods train would come down the line and have these trucks shunted off. Other merchandise, including horse manure from London stables for the local gardens would also come that way. The London and South Railway Company was an employer of local labour for signal men, porters and station masters in residence, all of which posts have disappeared. One of the local carriers was Mr Kent of Wormley who had horse drawn vans for this purpose; he was later followed by his son with a motor van. Also at Wormley, as a necessary adjunct to King Edward's School, was a gas works to supply the light and heating for the buildings there.

Mr Sparks' father collected the rubbish and emptied the ash bins in Milford with his horse and cart. The rubbish was used as the foundations for a new road behind the Stag Inn at Eashing down to the river where a barge was moored. The barge was used to collect sharp sand from the river bed. Mr Sparks' horse and cart were also used when the new road between Enton and Milford Hospital was built. He was paid £1.50 a day for its use. Mr Wattee, the tea planter who lived at Enton, gave Mr Sparks a donkey and trap. The donkey was popular with all the local children who used to come and ride it in the allotments and open fields that were at the end of Chapel Lane. The donkey felt itself to be one of the family, and would go into the house through the scullery and kitchen into the living room for meals. The large Shire horse had to content itself with putting its head through the window for tit-bits. His favourite was Woodbines cigarettes!

The National Laying Test Centre near Milford Station was another source of local employment. This centre later became the National Poultry Farm and then Marsh Farm before being sold in 1997 with plans for redevelopment as an angling centre. Mr Childs saw many of these changes, working there from 1934 until he retired. As the National Laying Test Centre, it attracted pedigree birds from around the country, all competing to see which was the best layer. The competitions were between pens of 6 or 12 birds, for single birds, 2 birds and 3 birds. The cups and prizes were promoted by the Daily Mail, whose owner Lord Northcliffe was a friend of one of the managing directors, J. N. Lee. Mr Lee had seen the site from the train and decided to move his poultry farm there from Bordon to build up the competitions. Once the Daily Mail no longer sponsored the trials, the business turned commercial and instead of pedigree birds, all sorts were tested for commercial egg production.

Education in Milford was provided in the village school in Church Road. Miss Cicely Puttick remembered when Mr Christmas was head-teacher, but he left to become secretary to a firm of publishers in Haslemere. He was succeeded by Mr J. W. Marsh who had the reputation of being a dedicated, hard-working head-teacher. Mr Sparks remembers that two boys were sent each day to the sweetshop and tobacconist for 20 Gold Flake cigarettes for their teacher. The boys would wait for them to be smoked and discarded and then they would collect the butts to smoke themselves. The late Mrs Bessie Puttick taught at the school when the head-teacher lived on the premises. The room that was known as the staff room in the 1950s had been a bedroom. The main part of that early school building has gone but part remains as the Lounge at Church Close. There had been another school in Milford at the end of the 19th century when a large house at the apex of the Petworth and Haslemere Roads, Highcroft, was a private school for boys. Highcroft was owned by Mrs Peachy who sold it for conversion into flats, keeping one for herself, before it was finally demolished to make way for the eponymous sheltered housing development on the site.

In Witley and the surrounding hamlets, there was King Edward's School, Witley School, which was started in 1836, and a small primary at Brook. As well as reading, writing and arithmetic, there was gardening for boys and sewing for girls. English grammar, poetry and the rudiments of musical notation were included at the village school, whilst King Edward's taught its boys useful trades such as carpentry and metalwork. Music featured strongly at King Edward's, encouraged by the Foster families of Sandhills. The military band was in great demand in the local area at Jubilees and Fetes and for leading Empire Day parades until 1926 when a change of regime put more emphasis on the science and technical departments, leaving just a drum and bugle band for community events.

Miss Ruth Mullard, who was a pupil there between the wars, recalls the heating at Witley School as rudimentary: a tall round iron coal stove in a corner of two classrooms and open coal fires in the other two. The infant teacher, Miss Cranstone, made a lasting impression on all her pupils. Miss Luff took the next class. She taught at the school for about 50 years, having

Milford School, ca 1913

started as a pupil teacher as soon as she herself left school and staying there until she retired. She drummed the basic skills of reading and writing into generations of Witley children. None left the school lacking these essentials. Daily drill was conducted in the area above the school by the hut. A highlight of the school year was Empire Day, May 24th. Children took red, white and blue flowers to school: campions, cow parsley and bluebells. After a service in church, the pupils came back and formed up to salute the Union Flag, singing 'I vow to thee my country' and the National Anthem. In the afternoon, the landlord of The White Hart, Mr Robert Holmes, gave the children a party with currant buns but no butter.

Behind the school the boys cultivated plots of vegetables which were regularly entered in the annual village show. The girls made dresses in needlework classes for their entries and all the children competed for the largest collection of wild flowers and grasses. The show was well supported as most people grew flowers and vegetables for it. Children's sports and a Fun Fair ensured its popularity with the children.

A succession of girl apprentices perfected their sewing skills by joining the small dressmaking business of Maud Ashdown Robes. It was first established in a hut by Wormley railway bridge and moved to The Larches where a large workroom was included in the plans when it was built in 1910. With such skills perfected the girls could secure good employment as children's or lady's maids. In Milford, Miss Denyer ran a dress-making establishment at Rose Cottage in New Road. Dolly Francis, who was born around 1898, told Mrs Heys that she remembered sewing in a room in the single storey part of the house. Most pupils left school at 14, unless they passed the exam to go to the County School in Godalming (now the 6th form College) for two more years. Many of the girls went into service in the large houses around.

National and local government both began to address the housing shortage and the sub-standard accommodation in many older properties. Twelve council dwellings were built in each village with more houses built for private rental or ownership. Churchfields and Roke Lane in Witley both started being developed in the 1920s. Many of the houses in Chapel Lane in Milford were built using demolition materials from the army camp on the common. Large houses continued to be built, including 'Brackens' on Wormley Hill that was built for the niece of William Gladstone.

The Witley and Milford Commons were grazed between the wars. The present level of tree cover is relatively recent as grazing maintained open heathland. There have always been some pine trees and the pine cones were gathered for firelighters. Percy Childs remembers going to the top of Rodborough Hill to see Crystal Palace burning down. Geoffrey Lawrence lived as a boy at number 7 Mare Hill and was responsible for grazing the family's goats. He remembers a day before the second world war when he was cutting grass in the valley and he saw smoke further up the hill. Someone passing on the Haslemere Road had tossed a cigarette end onto the heath, setting it ablaze. Mr Lawrence raced up the hill to round up and save his goats.

The commons were playgrounds for many of the local children who regularly blocked the outlet from the spring on Mare Hill so that a pool would form to bathe in. The stream across Station Lane in Milford was another popular paddling place. Sometimes the children were disturbed by the local otter hounds, chasing otters into the lake at Rake Manor. The children from the top of Witley village joined those from Culmer and spent whole days in the woods by Sweetwater, building houses with broken branches and bracken. Whortleberries and blackberries were picked in season, and taken home

Rodborough Common, from Oxted Green ca 1935

Milford Heath at the turn of the century: it remained relatively unchanged until after 1945

along with bags of fir cones. Frederick Sparks recalls the hours he and his friends spent in the underground tunnels left by the army on Rodborough Common. The artist Thackeray Turner gave much of the common to the National Trust in 1921, ensuring its continued enjoyment by future generations. Other pastimes were playing with whip tops, hoops and five stones, skipping and cats cradle. Most of the pavements had hopscotch markings on them. Scouts was well established, and there was a strong branch of the Girls Friendly Society. The younger people belonged to the Children's Union, established to raise money to help less fortunate children. Miss Mullard remembers being given sixpence to make things like kettle holders and egg cosies for sale to turn that sixpence into five shillings – 10 times as much.

Milford had a tennis court between the wars, opposite the chemist shop. Cricket and football have always been prominent and the Saturday afternoon cricket games were real village occasions. Witley Cricket Club was founded in 1869. Everyone, men, women and children came to what was still the Manor Park complete with picnics to support Witley's village team. Alternatively, meals from the White Hart were served in the British Legion. One popular event was the local Derby between Witley and Milford. Sunday Cricket did not start in Witley until after the war, instigated by a local electrician, Alfred Butler. Stumps had to be pulled by 5.30 in time for Evensong. Indoors, the Dramatic Society put on two plays a year: the Pantomime Company did not start until 1956. Professional drama came to the village in 1926 when the film 'Dick Turpin's Ride to York' was shot in Church Lane, using the White Hart and its staff in one scene. Witley Fair, held in the Manor Park on May 29th each year, was another well established event. Witley and District Motorcycle Club was started in Mullard's Yard and then transferred to Gore's Garage at Crossways, now the site of Baynards Motors.

A Fair and Sports were held on August Bank Holiday, which was then the first Monday in August, on a large field where Cherry Tree Road and Jubilee Field now stand. The previous Saturday was designated 'Hospital Saturday'. Mr Sparks senior decorated his horse and cart as a hospital ward and drove it round the village, collecting for the Royal Surrey Hospital which was then maintained entirely by subscriptions. Mr Sparks raised more money than anyone else and became a life member of the hospital. In the afternoon there was a children's fancy dress parade, assembling at

Moushill Green and ending on the Cricket Green. An evening dance in the cricket pavilion rounded off the day's events. The fair ran for about 50 years before a lack of volunteers to run it forced it to cease. Another fair was held annually at Moushill Manor. One year there was a donkey derby with a side of bacon as the prize. Fred Sparks entered his father's donkey, but the animal wouldn't budge an inch.

The ex-army huts were soon considered inadequate to meet the increasing social needs of both villages with Milford residents leading the way. In 1922, Archdeacon Beresford Potter of Rake Manor, commissioned the architect he was using at Rake, Baillie Scott, to design a new Women's Institute building in Portsmouth Road in Milford. The hall has some interesting similarities to the billiards room at Rake. Some of the necessary money was given by the Wattee tea family (after whom Mazzawattee tea was named) who lived at Enton Green, but Mrs Potter ensured the building was completed.

The original part of the building was known as Potter's Hall and was used for Bible Classes and other Church uses as well as meeting the increasing social and welfare needs of the village. The first caretaker lived in part of the Hall: the kitchen is now used as the Parish Council Offices. The bedroom was at the opposite end of the hall. The balcony served as another room. There was a clock donated by Mr Disney, the Postmaster, in memory of his daughter.

In 1927 the Institute was leased to the then Vicar of Milford, Rev Wanstall, for seven years at an annual rent of £2.00. It was forbidden to use the hall for any trade, business or auction, and there were signs expressly forbidding dancing, the playing of cards or other games for money, or the sale of intoxicating liquor. It was to be used solely for religious, educational, philanthropic or social purposes. In 1929, Mrs Potter assigned the property to be held in trust for the people of Milford and in 1930, it became a registered Charitable Trust.

Brook and Sandhills residents had no social centre of their own and many fund raising events were held in the Witley Hut, some organised by the active Brook and Sandhills Women's Institute. They raised over £500 for what was to become the Pirrie Hall. Lord Pirrie gave the land and had the Hall built for the benefit of residents of Brook and Sandhills in 1923. Since

Milford Village Hall as it is in 1999

1947, Brook Fete has been held annually on the Spring Bank Holiday, to maintain the Hall and the adjoining cricket ground.

Witley residents wanted a public recreation ground rather than having to rely on the goodwill of the landlord and tenant of Witley Manor for access to part of the Park. Although this access was not generally denied, it was decided to pursue the possibility of ensuring its continued use for villagers. Robert Holmes, who was the most influential figure in Witley, and Chairman of the Parish Council, negotiated with the Chandler family for part of the park. In 1932, the Parish Council signed a tenancy agreement with the landlord and tenant of Witley Manor to establish a recreation ground for the use of villagers, with the intention that this use should remain in perpetuity. The rent was set at a nominal fee. Subsequently, constructive improvements could be made, especially to the cricket area which no longer had to be cleared of Mr Stovold's grazing cows before play could start! A wooden pavilion served the needs of the sports clubs until a new village hall was proposed.

Like most projects of this kind, the decision to build had not been taken without certain misgivings. The Hall was to be located on part of the

Recreation Ground, and at one time it was believed that the local branch of the British Legion would be provided with an annex for its use with facilities for the sale of liquor. This did not go down too well with the members of the Parish Council at the time as it was considered by them to be most undesirable. The final design for the Hall was built by the local firm of F. Milton and Sons, on land purchased from the Chandler Trust with money provided by Mrs Spencer Chichester of Enton Hall in memory of Major Chichester. It was to seat 250 people, with basement accommodation for the cricket club and a verandah overlooking the adjoining pitch. Expert advice was sought on the acoustics and the luxury of an up-to-date electric gramophone with two amplifiers installed. According to a newspaper report, Mrs Chichester and her family took the 'closest interest in the scheme, making frequent inspections during the construction and equipment of the building.'

The formal handing over to the trustees representing the village was followed by an entertainment by The Play Makers of London to those inhabitants of 18 years and over within the ecclesiastical boundary of Witley. A certain number of seats were reserved for those contributing 2s 6d and a silver collection was taken on behalf of the Witley Nursing Association. The Hall was opened in January, in good time for the Silver Jubilee of King George V and Queen Mary. The Jubilee was celebrated with a peal of bells and a parade of floats and fancy dresses from the Star to the Recreation Ground, with each child given a Jubilee mug. A tea party was laid on in the Hall for all the children of Witley. There was a terrific thunderstorm: all the lights went out and there was no hot water for the washing up.

When war was declared in September 1939, everyone became busy filling sandbags and making blackout curtains. The local Red Cross ladies scrub-bed and cleaned the hall to make it ready for use as a casualty station. The Head Warden, Mr Edwards, had his headquarters in the stokehold (the boiler room) at the Hall, and each night he slept there in order to be ready for any emergency. At this time the Hall was not being used, but then the Canadians arrived. Dances were held in the Hall and continued thro-ughout the rest of the war, the local residents becoming accustomed to the 'drunk truck' coming along at the end of the evening to pick up the 'casualties'.

Among the strictures laid down by the original Deed of Trust is the responsibility laid on the Management Committee to preserve the letting of the Hall from a 'society or body promoting sentiments or propaganda of a disloyal, unpatriotic or seditious character' and to uphold the wishes of Mrs Chichester that no dance should be held on Armistice Night or Good Friday. Despite these restrictions the Chichester Hall, regarded when it was opened as one of the finest village halls in the South of England, continues to provide a home to many village events, including the now yearly pantomime.

Mr Holmes had again been instrumental in persuading the Chichester family to build the Hall, and he planted the copper beech tree in the recreation ground nearby. His granddaughter reckoned that he ran Witley as nothing happened without his support. Unless his name was at the top of the pledge list when it went round the big houses, no-one else would contribute to the cause. He moved into the White Hart in 1907, handing over the daily running of the hotel to his son Ayliffe in 1918. Ayliffe Holmes ran the inn until 1931 when he moved to Camberley, but Robert Holmes remained in Witley. Robert Holmes died in 1947, by which time he had been a school manager for 40 years, a churchwarden for 23 and on the Parish Council for 30 years, with several terms as chairman. He represented Witley on the Hambledon Board of Guardians and the Rural Council. His responsibilities to the workhouse included going over every Christmas Day to carve the turkeys. He sponsored two pupils at King Edward's School and was a very generous man, hosting frequent smoking parties in the British Legion. His birthday was Christmas Day, and each year he gave 2/6d to a local boy, Ronald Mott, who shared his birthday. The Holmes were a musical family, with Ayliffe playing the piano at all the dances in the village and singing over 70 solos in Church. At concerts in the Women's Hut, Robert played violin and Ayliffe the piano whilst both sang.

The White Hart was extended during his tenure, at the request of the many artists who visited Witley and wanted somewhere to stay. He built on the accommodation wing, so that there were 11 bedrooms in the hotel. The dining room offered silver service, Mr Holmes having been originally trained as butler to the Duke of Buccleugh. His expertise was passed onto a succession of trainees. During the war, Canadian officers used the hotel's accommodation. Mr Holmes built the first house on Culmer Hill, Hough-ton, and about a year later, a second one next door, Drayton. When he died these constituted his entire estate as he always gave away any money he had.

Medical services expanded between the wars. Dr Booker built another house, now the Witley Vicarage, in the grounds of his own for his partner Dr Blazeby. His son, 'young Dr Frederick' practised from his own house, Abbotsmead, at Culmer, serving the Wormley end of the village. All the doctors practised from their own homes until well into the 1960s when a purpose built surgery was opened in Roke Lane. At the same time, a receptionist was appointed to relieve the burden on the doctors' wives. With surgeries in their own homes, the houses could never be left unattended apart from the half day a week and one weekend a month that each doctor had off. No appointment system was operated, so surgeries sometimes continued until 9.30 at night. The Roke Lane Surgery is now the Dental Practice which took over the premises when a new surgery was built in Wheeler Lane in 1989.

In Milford, Wyndham Lodge in Church Road housed a succession of doctors. Dr Hall had an early model of a car with acetylene lamps. He employed a uniformed chauffeur, Mr Bird, but this gentleman couldn't drive! He sat in the front seat next to the doctor, who did all his own driving. The Milford branch of the Witley surgery at Milford Crossroads did not open until the 1960s.

Although very few people had motor cars, both the AA and RAC were represented in Milford. An RAC box was situated at the junction of Petworth Road and Church Road and Milford Crossroads, where there was a triangular patch of green, was the main AA position. The patrol man stood there all day directing traffic or going around on his motor bike, in spite of the fact that he only had one arm.

During the construction of the Godalming-Guildford by pass, a café on the corner of Cherry Tree and Portsmouth Roads, next to the garage, took coffee and cigarettes out to the construction workers. This café was popular with the local youngsters as you could get half a sardine on toast there for 1d. The Godalming to Guildford by-pass opened in 1934 and Manor Weald Service Station and café opened in that summer to cater for the new passing trade. It was designed by Charles Mitchell, a partner in the Godalming architectural firm of J. H. Norris. It was designed in the style of an imposing country house, with tall chimneys and 'eyebrows' over the windows owing much to the influence of the more famous Surrey architect, Sir Edwin Lutyens. Manor Weald Service Station was regularly used by Amy

Milford Crossroads and AA patrolman, ca 1917

'The Hill', with 'Stonehaven' and workmen's cottages to the right, and a pet's cemetery in the crescent in the garden to the left, ca 1939

Johnston (née Mollison) for petrol for her sports car. Charles Mitchell also designed a thatched petrol station on the bypass at Eashing, with twin turrets. Mitchell's buildings at Manor Weald were demolished by Esso in 1994, in spite of strong local opposition, to make way for a new two storey house. Eashing has fared slightly better, but only a little of the original building remains.

Chapter 5

The Second World War

By the time the second world war broke out, much of Witley and Milford considered itself quite sophisticated, with all "mod cons". The villages filled with evacuees: the women didn't like the quiet surroundings though the children adapted better. The Canadians came back to a new camp on the common, and the soldiers were frequent visitors to the local pubs. Mrs Talman got to know several of them quite well. Hers was the only telephone in the village, and many soldiers came across from the Star to ask if they could phone home to reassure their families. This time cricket prevailed on Milford Heath. The famous West Indian cricketer and statesman, Leary Constantine, played there against the local team.

The Canadian Government built three camps on Witley Common. One was around the present day National Trust Centre, one on Rodborough Common beyond Rodborough Hill and the third was beyond the cemetery as far as Webb Road. Each was like a small village, with chapels, a hospital, and the usual living accommodation. Each camp had its own parade ground, the remains of which are still very visible on the commons today. There was a large contingent of Polish troops in one camp. Their soldiers were responsible for the hawthorn planting around one of the parade grounds. Good roads served the vehicle areas of all camps. The Garrison theatre was a popular social centre for locals as well as troops, especially when films were shown or top ENSA stars came down from London. The Canadians were generally popular with the local populations, who found them very obliging and friendly. Their gifts were welcome too: Mr Sparks' family was given a whole round of cheese. He was on patrol on the common once with his lieutenant when they came across a man carrying a large bundle. They challenged him, and the man stumbled against the lieutenant. The bundle was a large block of butter that the man was carrying to his girl friend in Eashing. Unfortunately, some was smeared across the front of the officer's uniform!

In another incident, on 7th October 1942 a party of soldiers exercising on Hankley Common found a dried hand sticking out of the sand. Other parts of the body were discovered and Superintendent Webb immediately set up a guard. The Chief Constable, Major Nicholson and Detective Chief Superintendent Roberts of Surrey C.I.D. and Dr Keith Simpson examined the body with Ted Greeno from Scotland Yard. The victim was identified as Joan Pearl Wolfe, who had been living on the common in a wigwam built for her by a Canadian Indian called August Sangret stationed at Witley Camp. Sangret tried and convicted of the murder, was hanged at Wandsworth.

All Saints Church was used as an air raid shelter for the pupils at the school across the road. Mr Harry Swallow, the head-teacher, shepherded his charges across the road every time the air raid siren sounded. St John's in Milford was similarly used for the pupils from Milford School. The church was dark, with heavy deep red or dark blue curtains across the windows. The rails on which they hung still remain over the windows on the south side. When all the pupils were seated, community singing started. The children all enjoyed it, unaware of any possible implications of the raids. The disruption to lessons must have been very frustrating for the teachers, but Peggy Bookham remembers their dedication fondly and reckons many Milfordians owe them much. Miss Holloway, one of the teachers in the junior school, was a respected needlewoman. Her skills were not wasted on Peggy, who later became a needlework teacher herself. Schooling was very different then from now: one teacher had an uncanny aim with a rubber if someone was talking during lessons. A list of ten words would appear each Monday on the spelling blackboard, to be learnt ready for a test on Friday. Last lesson on Monday morning was 'Hygiene' when naughty girls who bit their finger nails were made to sit at the front of the class. On wet days, some children were regularly absent from school as their only pair of shoes let in water. Poverty and clothing rationing meant they had to wait their turn for a new pair.

Harry Swallow and the local police sergeant, Sgt Hagley, known by all as 'Sarge', were two local members of the Royal Observer Corp, plotting enemy aircraft over Witley. For a time during the war a telescope was mounted on the church tower to observe a light shining intermittently at night from St Dominic's School in Hambledon. As a result the operator of the light was arrested. One Heinkel aircraft came down in the grounds of King Edwards' School, with the engines falling into Sweetwater Pond. The crew were buried in Milford Cemetery. A bomb landed at Heaven's Gate on Rodborough Common and several exploded along Moushill Lane, completely missing the nearby column of tanks in what is now the service road along Cherry Tree Road.

The Red Cross had a First Aid Centre at Witley Manor and the Civil Defence used the basement of the Chichester Hall as their headquarters. Luckily there were few casualties. A bomb on the Common landed just before the Canadians moved in only killing a rabbit and one was dropped near Enton Hall but again before the troops moved in. There were plenty of enemy planes overhead, flying through the Shoreham gap on their way to London. Anti-aircraft guns were active, usually in the distance, and some planes were shot down whilst others jettisoned their bombs. A land mine dropped near Gorse Hill, and a doodle bug demolished Winkford Lodge, slightly injuring the gardener. The blast was strong enough to turn over the desks in Witley School. Shortly after the end of hostilities in Europe, an evacuee in Witley saw an RAF plane overhead. No sooner had he thought "At least you're safe now" than he heard the engine note change and saw the plane plummet from the sky. The New Zealand crew were buried in Witley Churchyard but on a return visit 50 years later, that evacuee could not find the grave and thought the bodies had been later returned to New Zealand.

In June 1940, 200 French boys between the ages of 14 and 16, escaping from German occupation, were billeted at Rake Manor. All the stables and outbuildings were used to accommodate personnel. They soon formed part of the School of Military Cadets of Free France, under the overall control of General de Gaulle. The General came to review the cadets, and a contingent of the local Home Guard, in December 1940. Their tenure of Rake was short lived, as in February 1941 the cadets were transferred to Malvern School. Graffiti on the outside door of the billiard room remains as a relic of the French occupancy of Rake.

King Edward's School's capacious buildings were also used for the war effort. The Admiralty Signal Establishment requisitioned it for scientific research between 1942 and 1948. The inevitable reduction of pupil numbers during the war meant that they could be accommodated in smaller premises and they moved to the Institution building (the old workhouse) at Hambledon. A plaque in the school records that during its time at Witley, the Admiralty researchers, "developed British Naval Radar which was used with great effect in the Battle of the Atlantic, in the sinking of the Scharnhorst and in many other naval operations." Amongst those researchers were Sir Fred Hoyle, Sir Hermann Bondi and Professor Tommy Gould.

Many evacuees came to the villages during the war, both individuals and businesses. 'Sherborne', near Witley Wines, was one of many houses around that took in evacuees, but one of its bedrooms was fitted with a sink and its own gas supply. This room was used as a refuge by Jews fleeing from Europe to other towns in England. De Beer's diamond company transferred its offices to Wo Yuen at Enton, the home of the Massa Wattee family with Enton Mill occupied by the Scottinsh Boiler and General Insurance Company. Pitchin and Johnson, the paint company, took over 'The Hill' on Wormley Hill. Competition for empty houses for the staff of all these firms was fierce. One of the largest establishments that moved here away from the London Blitz was St Thomas' Hospital which was promised the use of a hutted hospital adjoining the King George V Sanatorium at Hydestile. The huts had been used by Commonwealth troops as the 'Third Australian General Hospital'. When these troops moved out, arrangements were made for essentials like the X-ray department, laboratories, residential accommodation, (two large houses in Milford), the Nurses Training School (which occupied Manor House in Godalming) and transport for the nurses to and from the new hospital. Warner's Coach Company of Milford provided this service throughout the war.

Two wards were ready for the first patients in April 1941, the day after the Lambeth site suffered from one of the worst raids of the war. Incendiary bombs destroyed much of the fabric of the hospital, delaying the start of transfer of the first 20 patients to the safety of Hydestile. Convoys of patients came down weekly as new accommodation was made ready for them so that by August 1941, 268 beds were occupied. The supply logistics to the number of sites that now accommodated parts of St Thomas' were complex. Even transporting the bedsteads posed problems as the first consignment arrived at Hydestile as separate stacks of heads, feet and centres. Only then was it found to be a false assumption that all these were of a standard pattern! There were slight differences of fitting and not every head and foot would connect with every centre. Vegetables still came from Covent Garden to Hydestile, with fruit coming from the hospitals' own farms in Essex. A fish canning factory near Colchester agreed to can the fruit and about 2,000 gallon tins containing nearly 12,000 pounds of fruit, were prepared each year during the war.

By 1943 there were 334 beds in Hydestile, nearly twice as many as in Lambeth, and it remained as a fully operational teaching hospital until 1950. After then, as departments were transferred gradually back to the reconstructed Lambeth site, Hydestile was wound down although some activities remained there until 1968 when it was finally closed.

Albert Edwards ran a mobile tea shop near Milford Station which catered for visitors to the three hospitals (St Thomas', King George V and Milford Chest) as they got off the train. His mobile canteen was a regular feature at football and cricket matches and the Saturday night dances at Chichester Hall both during and after the war. Reginald (Dick) Harvey worked and lived at the Poultry Farm during the war. He was approached by the almoner at St Thomas' to accommodate visitors to some of their patients. One of them, noticing the wonderful array of flowers in Dick's garden, suggested to him that he sold bunches of them on Milford Station for visitors to take up to the hospitals. The first Sunday, this task was entrusted to his 9 year old son, but was so successful that he was deemed to be too young to be entrusted with so much money. Other family members were enlisted and for the rest of the war, Saturday evenings in summer were devoted to cutting and bunching flowers which were sold at 1/6d a bunch.

Witley's vicar, the Rev Holden, was also chaplain to Milford Chest and King George V Hospitals. He went everywhere by bike and never failed to turn out to minister the last rites to a patient at the hospitals. The chest hospital had many TB cases, and call outs were frequent. By the end of the war, he was in his 70s. He had a rota for his parochial visits so that every household was visited at least once a year, whether or not they were church goers. The vicar's wife and daughter cycled to work at Haslemere hospital each day.

One bitterly cold day in the winter of 1946/7 the Rev Holden came upon young Ron Mott leaving the White Hart. Having spent 14 years in the choir, Ron was well known to the vicar who expressed his pleasure at seeing him returned from the war, especially as he had been wounded in 1941. The vicar proceeded to tell Ron of a mysterious phantom of Witley Churchyard. Following a tragic accident involving a glass window, a young schoolgirl, Mary, of about 12 years old had died and was buried in the churchyard. Now it was an unfortunate fact that the graves had become overgrown; however, a few weeks previous to this meeting, Mary's grave had been cleared and fresh flowers arranged there every week. Some time later, a woman had been seen tending the grave and when questioned, replied that she was a florist from Godalming who had been paid five shillings a week by an anonymous benefactor to tend the grave but the money was now used up. The phantom was laid to rest and the benefactor never disclosed.

Peggy Bookham (née Reeves) was a child during the war. Her family moved to Milford from Witley in 1940 when Peggy was 8. Her father went to work at Jordan's garage (now White's). He had been a chauffeur but his employer, like many others, could no longer afford such a luxury. The garage maintained cars and lorries for essential services. It was a reserved occupation, so Peggy's father joined the auxiliary fire service, sleeping at the fire station in Witley every third night throughout the war. He attended the aftermath of several 'doodle bugs' that landed in this area. Witley Fire Station crew were often called up to Esher to cover that area when the firemen from Esher were called to help in London during the air raids. The family lived in an asbestos bungalow behind the garage on land now occupied by the car showroom. The garage was taken over by the army during the war, firstly by the Queen's Bays, then the Canadians and finally by R.E.M.E. The service road along Cherry Tree Road was used for storing and maintaining tanks, so the road was called the 'Tank Trap'. Fields were where the houses now stand and the cherry trees were very small. Soldiers were billeted in many of the large houses around, including Milford Lodge House, four Victorian houses that used to stand on the Haslemere road and Eagle House in New Road. The gate posts at the lower entrance to Milford Lodge were soon damaged by tanks.

One of Peggy's earliest recollections was going with the rest of the Brownies into the black barn opposite Blackhill Pond to sort waste paper. The barn was full of it, and the little girls clambered all over it to 'help' with the sorting and the war effort. With hindsight, she wondered if they were more of a hindrance than a help. Guides in Milford closed during the war, but some of the girls continued their Guiding at Witley. Because of the black out, meetings were held directly after school. The Robin patrol had to meet on Saturday mornings for those who went to Godalming County School or Guildford Technical College and could not get to the afternoon meetings. The Guide Captain, Joey Makovski, went into the MTC so her mother took over the company. The Saturday morning meetings were held in her house, Brook Cottage in Brook.

Peggy Bookham visited the camps regularly towards the end of the war, helping deliver newspapers on Saturday mornings and during the school holidays with Mrs Heather who ran the newsagents in Church Road that is now T. E. Francis. Mrs Heather's heavily laden car covered a sizeable round, including Culmer, Winkford and Parsonage Farms, Brook, Park Lane and out to Creedhole Farm which was then a convent. From there it went to Bowlhead Green and then to the camps. It took from 7 a.m. until 11 or 12 noon to complete the round.

There were very few cars on the roads, only those with essential work like doctors or those who were allowed a limited amount of petrol to shop. This was restricted to those who had no regular bus service or for some of the elderly and infirm. Everyone else had to disconnect the rotor arm from their car and deposit it at the local Police Station. Some of the young people passed the time car spotting: ten private vehicles in half an hour was good going. At night the headlights had to be virtually covered to comply with blackout regulations. Few people ventured far after dark. A popular pastime was 'Monopoly' which had come out just before the war and, played seriously, could occupy many a long evening. Peggy Bookham played regularly with her neighbours, John and Mary Wakeham. Their games would last for days, breaking only for meals or bedtime. John Wakeham went on to become a leading politician. He was injured in the Brighton bomb explosion and made a life peer on retiring from the House of Commons, becoming Chairman of the Press Complaints Commission.

There were many wartime weddings between English girls and the troops from overseas. One memorable one was between Phyllis Agar, the daughter of the owners of the local fish and chip shop, and a Canadian. Many of the young girls always gathered round the outside of the church to watch the weddings and hers was unusually pretty for war-time. The bride wore a long white dress and was attended by four bridesmaids also in long dresses, two in bright pink and two in deep purple satin. It was assumed that these had been sent from Canada, although it was possible to hire wedding attire to save on clothing coupons.

On the night before D-Day, many villagers gathered on Moushill Green by the fish and chip shop to watch hundreds of aircraft towing two gliders apiece on their way to the D-Day landings. The fish and chip shop did a roaring trade with both locals and the Canadians during the war as fish was not rationed.

A Land Army Hostel was established at Milford Crossroads where Rothwell's butcher's shop had been. An extension was built on the back to make an upstairs flat for the Warden. Churchill visited the Land Girls at one point during the war. One of the Land Girls became the village milkman. She drove a horse and cart around the village and across to Moushill corner. Peggy Bookham often went with her before she was old enough for the paper round. In return for her help, she was given a pint of milk for which her mother was very grateful. Another of Peggy's tasks was to go to a downstairs room in the hostel to buy a 4d mutton pie. These were only available once a week, and had to be ordered a week in advance.

National Savings Week was one of the events when all the village came together. A target sum was set for "Navy Week" or "Salute the soldier" or "Wings for Victory". There was a Carnival with a procession and Carnival Queen – for many years Pamela Blofeld who lived along the Portsmouth Road. Everyone decorated their houses with flags: Mrs Bookham's mother hung lengths of red, white and blue flag material from the office window that could be seen from the Portsmouth Road. She also placed a vase of pink campions, white cow parsley and bluebells on the table in the window. Various other activities were held during the week, including a dance at the Village Hall.

V.E. Day was celebrated in style. Peggy Bookham and Mary Wakeham went to Heather's newsagents and bought red white and blue ribbons which they sewed all round their white dresses. Peggy's was a hand-down from a cousin who had worn it for her Confirmation. There was a procession round the village, when everyone carried lighted torches. On VJ Day there was a service of Thanksgiving in St John's Church. In Witley, there was a procession of decorated floats through the village when the troops came home.

Chapter 6

Post War Development

Life changed again after the war with housing developments, both public and private, enlarging the local populations, but diminishing the rural aspect and employment opportunities within the area. The first council houses had gone up in Roke Lane between the wars, and the 1950s saw extensive building in Sunny Hill, Sunny Down and Croft Road. Private developments followed in the 60s and 70s so that by 1975 Witley was described by its Vicar, Philip Case, as a "divided village". He said that there were the old families who were born and bred in Witley, many of whom now lived in the council estates, and who supported each other, and the "incomers" who were either buying and renovating the old properties as the old inhabitants died off, or were moving into the new estates. Many of the newcomers chose to come to Witley because of its accessibility by road and rail, and because it had state schooling from 5 to 16 and private schools within its boundaries. Many commuted to London and had little time left for village affairs. Rev Case and his wife made many attempts to organise activities that would bond the two elements in village life, with limited success. They were not alone in recognising this division: Mrs Talman agreed, but thought that the village was more of a community again by the mid 90s, partly perhaps because there have been no large scale building projects for over 10 years as development land is limited.

Market gardens successively became housing estates, and the large houses could no longer maintain staff numbers at their pre-war levels. Ownership of Moushill Green, Milford Heath and the Pleck was transferred for a nominal sum from the estate of the Webb family of Milford House to Witley Parish Council in 1948. In the same year, Enton Hall became a health resort specialising for many years in dietetic and osteopathic treatments. When that business was no longer viable, it was converted into luxury apartments with an extension added in character with the original building. Many of the large houses that had once been home to the artistic community reflected the changing demography of the area by becoming residential nursing homes. Witley Park is a conference centre.

The Pleck in 1998 after excavation of wetland scrape as part of Witley Parish Council's management programme

Milton's Yard closed in 1985 after 110 years in the village, with some of its land used to build George Eliot Close. The buildings associated with the business have been converted into small business units.

Other places of employment have come and gone. The Institute of Oceanography moved into a site adjacent to King Edward's School in Wormley in 1953 when the Admiralty Signals Establishment moved to Portsdown. The Institute's research into marine science included developing the world renowned sonar system, Gloria, that maps the ocean floor. The Institute moved to Southampton in 1995, affiliating to the University's Marine Biology department.

Milford's shopping facilities expanded in the early 1950s when the Edwards family took over the premises at Crossroads that were no longer needed by the Land Army. Mr Edwards' old depot for his mobile canteen, by Milford Vicarage opposite Milford Heath, retained its link with refreshments by becoming the Café in the Trees, which survived into the 1970s. Mr Edwards was responsible for the rest of the parade being built so his grocery shop was soon joined by a butcher again, Mr Pride. Pride's specialised in pork and his sausages had a very good reputation locally. Mr Edwards himself died in 1969 and his business was sold a few years later. The shop has changed hands several times since, but still operates as a general store, now as part of the 'Alldays' chain. A notable new retailer in the village has been the Secrett family, with the farm shop and garden centre both opening during the 1970s and expanding into new ventures ever since.

Church Road, Milford ca 1965

Witley has fared worse than Milford and has gradually lost most of its retail outlets. The bike shop was the first to go from the parade by the lane to Enton Fisheries, but the rest closed or changed use during the 1970s, in spite of the increased population. The only unit that is still retail premises is the hairdresser. Witley Wines came to the village in 1984, originally in the old sweetshop, now the hairdressers, by which time there was no other grocery outlet in the village. Forrest Stores became a carpet shop but this too closed in the early 90s. Rawlinson's nursery is the sole surviving outlet for fruit and vegetables, although these are no longer produced on the premises. The general store on the corner of Crossways is now a basket shop. T. E. Francis still survives and has expanded its range into general items as well as those traditionally associated with a newsagents. Witley lost its Post Office in 1990, despite vigorous lobbying to keep it. Fortunately Wormley and Milford have both kept theirs.

Education facilities changed after the war with the Education Acts. Witley and Milford Schools were for the 5-11 year old children, who then went on to Godalming Grammar, Guildford Technical School or Rodborough Secondary Modern, which opened in 1952 in a series of huts on Rodborough Hill. Rodborough moved in 1960 to its present site on land that had belonged to Pleck Farm. Within a few years, the growing population meant that the buildings were inadequate. Extra 'moveable' classrooms were provided, and in 1968 the school was able to take over the vacant Civil Defence Buildings on the opposite side of the Petworth Road for the increasing numbers of fifth and sixth formers. In 1969 a standard design building, the two storey ROSLA unit, was provided in readiness for the raising of the school leaving age to 16 in 1972. A swimming pool was added to the school's facilities in 1971. Further expansion plans were thwarted by that familiar reason, budgetary restraints.

In the mid 70s, Surrey County Council changed its transfer ages again, and a new Middle School was built in Witley, Chandler School for 8-12 year olds. Witley and Milford Schools were left with the 5-8s and sixth form education was removed to specialist centres. Twenty years later it was change time again, with the Infant Schools expanding to take 4 year olds but losing their 8 year olds to the Junior School, which in turn passed them onto Rodborough at 11. Roke House was sold a few years after the war to a Catholic Order, the Josephites, who started a preparatory school for boys there, Barrow Hills School. In the early 90s, the Josephites left the school, which is now run by parent-trustees. In the grounds are still the vestiges of a Gertrude Jekyll garden. The chapel at Barrow Hills was the first place of worship for Roman Catholics in the Parish but in 1971, a new Catholic Church opened in Milford.

The provision and fortunes of social facilities has fluctuated in the last half of the 20th century. By 1964, Milford Village Hall was in need of modernisation and extension. Early plans were very ambitious, including the provision of a health centre. Fund raising and grants allowed construction of less ambitious, revised plans to begin in 1971, extending the hall to its present size. It is still central to village life, accommodating many educational, social and leisure activities for all ages from babies upwards. A new office was built onto the back of the Hall as an office for the Parish Council, reflecting its increasing workload and the demand for space. In 1998, the Parish Council office moved into a larger unit at the front of the hall, again reflecting its increasing responsibilities. Chichester Hall has also shown signs of wear and tear, but thanks to an enthusiastic management committee has succeeded in modernising and repairing the building on an ongoing basis since 1990. Pirrie Hall is trying to extend to meet its sporting commitments. The football and cricket clubs have worked hard to provide a suitable pavilion on Milford Heath. The 1930s building was extended in 1978, but twenty years later was inadequate. The advent of the lottery has made it possible to provide a much larger pavilion, extending its facilities to new user groups. This pavilion should be completed during 2000.

Youth clubs have also fluctuated in their fortunes, reflecting changing lifestyles both for the young people themselves and for those who volunteer to provide these services. Scouts has closed in Witley, although cubs, brownies and guides have managed to survive in both villages. In 1971, work started to provide a purpose built youth centre in Witley which opened in 1974. It has been used ever since by the football club, and over the years by playgroups and parent and toddler groups. It benefited from a refit in 1998.

Other organisations have had similar fates, some surviving, some changing and others combining. The only Women's Institute left in the parish now is at Milford, which started in 1964, whereas the older Brook and Sandhills and Witley branches have both closed. Golf has expanded with some of Secrett's land sold for Milford Golf Club in the early 90s.

The elderly members of the population have been catered for with the provision of some sheltered housing. The Dower House conversion in 1970 was one of the first in the Borough. A Day Centre opened in 1986, using the Milford Scout Hut for twelve years until a purpose built building was opened in Chapel Lane in 1998.

Tourism is the growth industry of the late 20th century, but the provision of the necessary associated infrastructure has declined. The cafés featured in many of the pre-war postcards of Milford no longer exist. Witley Manor and Milford House were both hotels in the immediate post war years, but now both are private residences. Milford House was destroyed by fire in the early 80s and was only restored and converted into apartments in 1999. At the other end of the accommodation scale, The Firs Youth Hostel opposite Milford Heath closed in the mid 1970s with the land used for housing. The Café in the Trees and Kay's Café in Witley both closed around the same time, although the parish is still well provided with pubs that serve food.

Milford House Luxury Apartments shortly after completion of conversion work in 1999

In 1977, Witley's vicar, Philip Case, chaired an energetic committee which organised a comprehensive programme to celebrate Queen Elizabeth II's Silver Jubilee. Every part of the Parish was involved, and there was something for every age group over the four days of varied events. Flower festivals decorated both parish churches and a civic service was held at All Saints, preceded by a peal of bells. In Milford the over 70s had a party and the Autumn Club organized a Jubilee fair and fancy dress show for all Parish children. Both villages had a procession of carnival floats that met at Rodborough School. There were rambles on the common, and a junior treasure hunt and barbecue. For the energetic there was a choice of amateur boxing, a spoon drive at the bowling club, cricket, it's a knockout and tugs of war. On the music side, there was a disco, a barn dance, a sing-along and a musical display. Pub games, Morris dancing, Brook Fete, a pet show with a child dog handling competition and a cycle relay race completed the programme. In 1982, Witley Parish Council was able to complete the villages' celebrations by purchasing Jubilee Field in Milford.

In 1995, the 50th anniversary of VE Day was celebrated with a fair at Witley Recreation Ground that was so popular, the organisers held a fair on August Bank Holiday Monday for the next three years. The proceeds all went to local organisations and causes.

As we move into the 21st century, it is surprising to see how many of the issues that concerned residents in the early part of the 20th century are still current preoccupations. Complaints about the volume and speed of traffic on the main roads have been joined by similar concerns on the many new residential streets that have grown up in the second half of the 20th century and are used as 'rat runs'. The cycle of increasing car ownership, declining village services and reduced public transport is hard to break, leaving those without access to either a car or public transport increasingly isolated. In 1999, the Parish Council started a community bus service on a weekly basis to take such people into Godalming and return them to their own front doors.

More surprisingly, residents in parts of Wormley, Brook and Sandhills still rely on cesspits for sewage. Vigorous campaigning for connection to a main sewerage system has had limited success, with some properties included in a nearby extension of sewerage in parts of Hambledon. For others, the only progress has been that the cesspits are no longer restricted to sink waste. Electricity, welcomed in the 1930s, was notoriously unreliable until after the major storm of October 1987. The supply comes from overhead cables that go through woods. Many of the trees and branches that had previously brought down power lines on moderately windy days either fell in the storm or were cleared during the efforts to reconnect everyone's supply. Parts of the parish were without power for 10 days.

The lovely commons that surround our parish are owned and managed for public enjoyment by Waverley Borough Council, Surrey County Council, the National Trust and English Nature. The National Trust opened an Information Centre at Witley in 1976 which is popular with schools from a wide area who visit its displays and go on guided walks. The commons too have changed during the past 100 years, from open heathland with specimen trees to areas of mixed woodland dominated by larger areas of birch, Scots pine and bracken. All the management bodies are now endeavouring to reclaim some of the heathland, to make a significant continuous area of the lowland heath that has been a rapidly disappearing habitat throughout Europe. Their success can be seen by the reappearance of flowers, insects and birds unique to this habitat. Our commons are now home to a number of species on the endangered lists. They also provide a welcome respite for local residents from the frenetic pace of life at the turn of the millennium.